THE HEYDAY OF East Kent

Ian Allan PUBLISHING

Glyn Kraemer-Johnson and John Bishop

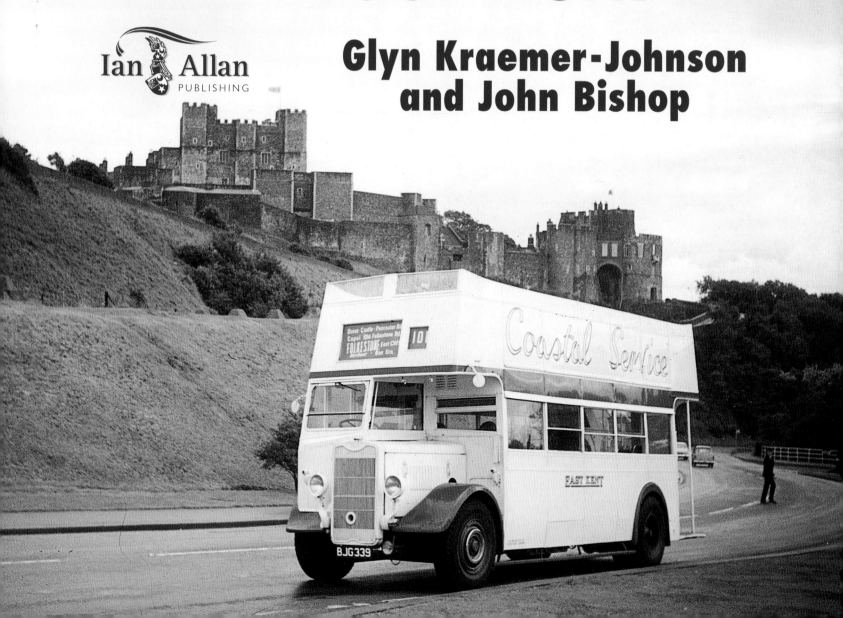

Front cover: Bound for Margate on route 52, AEC Regent V/Park Royal PFN 853 passes the 'Admiral Harvey' public house in Ramsgate in November 1963. Also worthy of mention are the classic British cars, a Mark II Ford Consul in particular capturing the essence of the 1960s. *John Allpress / John Bishop collection*

Back cover: East Kent had a small garage in the East Sussex town of Rye, and during the summer the station was a haven for its buses. Taking centre stage here is 36ft AEC Reliance OFN 717F of 1968, with the later style of BET-designed Marshall bodywork, while on the left are two earlier, shorter Reliances with dual-purpose Weymann bodywork. *Rob Crouch*

Previous page: With Dover Castle as a backdrop, Guy Arab/Park Royal BJG 339 waits to depart on the arduous run to Folkestone. New in 1944, it was converted to open-top in 1960, continuing to serve the company until 1968. *Rob Crouch*

Left: Canterbury can always guarantee a picturesque view, no matter what vehicle is portrayed. Passing through the West Gate is Park Royal-bodied AEC Regent V GJG 747D of 1966, the rather lurid rear advertisement marring an otherwise pristine vehicle. *Howard Butler*

Introduction by Glyn Kraemer-Johnson
Photographs selected and captioned by John Bishop

First published 2007

ISBN (10) 0 7110 3206 8
ISBN (13) 978 0 7110 3206 4

Published by Ian Allan Publishing

an imprint of Ian Allan Publishing Ltd, Hersham, Surrey, KT12 4RG.
Printed in England by Ian Allan Printing Ltd, Hersham, Surrey, KT12 4RG.

Code: 0711/B1

Visit the Ian Allan Publishing website at www.ianallanpublishing.com

Introduction

It operated what must be amongst the most handsome double-deckers ever built — Park Royal-bodied Guy Arab IVs delivered in 1956/7 and bearing 'MFN' registrations. They were of the same basic type as was delivered to Southdown Motor Services at around the same time, but, whilst the interior specification of the Southdown vehicles was to a higher standard, in external appearance the East Kent examples had the edge. Their four-bay construction (as opposed to Southdown's five-bay) gave them a sleeker appearance, and their concealed radiators or 'tin fronts', generally frowned upon by enthusiasts, formed an integral part of the overall design, unlike the collection of headlamps, mudguards and grille of the exposed-radiator version, which appeared to have been 'stuck on' to the graceful contours of the body.

The MFNs were the last of a long line of Park Royal-bodied Guys that had originated with the utility designs of World War 2. Like some other operators, such as Chester and, to a lesser degree, Southdown, East Kent had been impressed by the rugged reliability of the Arab and had adopted it as standard throughout the 'Forties and early 'Fifties.

East Kent's association with Park Royal stretched back even further, to 1932, when a batch of unusual Morris Commercial Imperial double-deckers was delivered to the company. There were a few 'blips' over the years, such as the all-Leyland PD1s bought in 1946, when new buses were in short supply and it was a case of 'taking what you could get' to replace war-weary and time-expired buses. To help further a number of prewar Leyland TD4s was rebodied, the work being shared between Park Royal and Eastern Coach Works, but, in the main, Park Royal remained the chosen bodybuilder right through until the 'Seventies, when the National Bus Company's corporate vehicle policy brought the Leyland National and Bristol VR into the fleet.

Apart from the Morris Commercials, Leyland double-deckers had been favoured before World War 2, but when the Arab ceased to be available the AEC Regent became the standard double-decker. First came the handsome full-fronted 'Puffins' (the name being derived from their PFN registrations), to be followed by half-cab versions with somewhat ungainly Park Royal bodies derived from the Bridgemaster.

Right: The London–Brighton Historical Commercial run in 1991 was a wet one, but the visit was worthwhile with the outing of preserved Brush-bodied Tilling-Stevens JG 669. Just visible is another Park Royal-bodied East Kent vehicle to the left. Restorations like this make one marvel at the dedication and resourcefulness of their respective owners. *John Bishop*

Single-deckers and coaches followed much the same pattern, prewar deliveries being mainly of Leyland manufacture. During the 'Forties and early 'Fifties the company showed a predilection for the Dennis Lancet before turning to the AEC Reliance for the bulk of its underfloor-engined chassis, although here too there were the odd men out — Leyland Royal Tigers, Commer-Beadle integrals, a handful of Bedfords and even a Ford Thames Trader. As with the 'deckers, Park Royal bodied the majority, but again there were exceptions, such as the Beadle-bodied coaches of the mid-'Fifties, the touring-coach version being another firm favourite of the authors.

East Kent's livery of crimson and ivory was both smart and attractive and did much to enhance the appearance of its vehicles. It even gave a certain elegance to the ungainly half-cab Regent Vs, whose Park Royal bodies were a far cry from the subtle curves of the MFNs. Moreover, it complemented the dark green and cream and apple green and cream of sister companies Maidstone & District and Southdown.

The East Kent Road Car Co Ltd was a company of considerable interest and individuality. Even the title 'Road Car Company' (something it shared with West Yorkshire and Lincolnshire) seemed to lend it an air of superiority. As has already been demonstrated, although part of the British Electric Traction group it pursued an individualistic vehicle policy.

It was also unusual in that it had no fleet-numbering system, the registration number being used for identification purposes. Furthermore, its operating territory, tucked away in the southeasternmost corner of the country, meant that during World War 2 the company was virtually in the front line, the Germans being able to shell Dover from their gun sites on the French coast. It also meant that the company was very much involved in the transporting of troops, particularly following the evacuation of Dunkirk.

In more recent times the importance of Dover as a ferry port also had its effect on East Kent with large numbers of vehicles being painted in ferry operators' colours for the transport of passengers between the station and the Docks. Another of East Kent's innovative operations was the coach-air service, inaugurated in conjunction with Skyways, whereby passengers travelled from London's Victoria Coach Station to Lympne Airport by East Kent coach before flying to Beauvais Airport (on the outskirts of Paris) by Skyways aircraft. The journey to Paris itself was again by coach. The company also linked with Europabus in 1953 to operate a through service from London to Frankfurt, the journey being by East Kent coach to Dover, ferry to Ostend and Europabus coach to Frankfurt. A number of East Kent coaches were painted in the pale blue Europabus livery for this service. However, perhaps the most adventurous operation was one in conjunction with

British Rail's Seaspeed hovercraft service, whereby East Kent coaches were actually transported across the English Channel by hovercraft, enabling the company to operate day tours to Northern France.

Northumberland is often described as 'the forgotten corner of England', but in terms of bus operation this epithet could be applied to East Kent, for, in spite of its history, its individuality and its innovative approach, the company seems for some reason to have been neglected by the enthusiast, and it is hoped that this volume will go some way towards redressing the balance.

For the purpose of this book, we have taken the 'Heyday' to be the period from the end of World War 2 to the absorption of the company into the National Bus Company, following which individuality and innovation disappeared along with that rich crimson and ivory and much local pride. The availability of colour photographs means that the coverage is mainly concentrated in the 'Sixties and early 'Seventies, with just a few from a little later.

We hope that this volume and its illustrations will bring back memories of a company for which we have a great fondness and admiration.

Glyn Kraemer-Johnson
Hailsham, East Sussex
March 2007

The mid-1970s saw most vehicles of the National Bus Company painted either leaf green or poppy red, so it was left to special occasions or preserved vehicles to remind us of the heyday of the East Kent Road Car Co. On 29 June 1975 the Southdown Enthusiasts' Club visited the Medway Towns and north Kent. The vehicle used was the Maidstone & District and East Kent Bus Club's preserved lowbridge all-Leyland Titan PD1, CJG 959. *John Bishop / Online Transport Archive*

Left: The lowbridge body of Park Royal-bodied Guy Arab III EFN 182 is shown to good effect in bright sunshine in this mid-1960s view. The location is the open area of Ashford garage, the bus having worked in on local Ashford route 121. Delivered in 1950, it would see service for 17 years before being sold for preservation in 1968. *Howard Butler*

Above: A sadly neglected aspect of bus photography is the rear view. However, this is addressed in this mid-1960s shot of a lowbridge Guy Arab with Park Royal bodywork. Canterbury bus station is the location for EFN 179 on layover betweeen journeys on route 22, which at this time ran only on Wednesdays and Saturdays. The advertisement below the rear window for 'Rootes Service' harks back to the days of British car manufacture. *Howard Butler*

Above: A view of Canterbury, the heartland of the East Kent Road Car Company. Park Royal Guy Arab EFN 180, dating from 1950, is seen on the half-hourly route from Mandeville Road to Barton Road, alternate journeys being extended into Barton Estate in the mid-1960s, when this photograph was taken; note the collars and ties then in vogue. EFN 180 would be sold for scrap in 1966, enabling us to date this view fairly accurately. *Howard Butler*

Right: Park Royal-bodied Guy Arab EFN 178, dating from 1950, squeezes through the West Gate in Canterbury on weekday route 23A in October 1963. Just visible through the arch is another bus of the same type, heading towards the bus station. *John Allpress / John Bishop collection*

A front nearside study of lowbridge Park Royal-bodied Guy Arab EFN 179, dating from 1950, in Canterbury bus station. The type's distinctive flared front mudguards are shown to good effect, as is the contemporary semaphore indicator.

Alongside is Weymann-bodied AEC Reliance KFN 248 of 1955. Finally withdrawn in 1967, EFN 179 would be scrapped the following year. *Howard Butler*

It would appear that the planners of Canterbury bus station had bus photographers in mind, judging from this comparative view. Until 1950 most East Kent double-deckers had lowbridge bodywork. However, the Park Royal-bodied Guy Arab IIIs delivered the following year, exemplified by FFN 365, sported highbridge bodywork. Alongside is Guy Arab IV GFN 919, with 'tin-front' enclosed radiator. *Howard Butler*

Above: Interestingly, while most of the 'GFN' class Park Royal-bodied Guy Arabs were delivered in 1953, GFN 908 was delivered in 1952. Even more surprising is that its bodywork was manufactured by Guy Motors and was originally mounted on a Guy Arab III chassis for display at the 1952 Commercial Motor Show. The vehicle was originally destined for the Newport Corporation. However, the order was cancelled and the body was fitted to the Arab IV, as depicted here, part of an order for 30 vehicles, the rest being bodied by Park Royal. *Howard Butler*

Right: At the lower end of Canterbury bus station is a Guy Arab IV, registered GFN 936, and showing the design innovation which gave rise to the 'tin front'. The elegant rake of the bodywork is clearly influenced by the London Transport RT class, and East Kent's classic livery sets the whole ensemble off perfectly. This vehicle was withdrawn in 1969 and went on to to see further service until being scrapped in 1973. *Howard Butler*

Above: Pursued by an AEC Regent V of the YJG batch, Guy Arab IV GFN 908 makes its way to Deal on route 66, which operated from Ramsgate via Sandwich. On the left, beyond the petrol station offering Pink Stamps, can be seen a Lambretta scooter, while jockeying for position behind the Guy is a smart Ford Anglia. *Rob Crouch*

Right: Resting between duties on city route 23, Guy Arab IV GFN 916 stands in Canterbury bus station, the well-proportioned lines of its four-bay Park Royal bodywork being shown to full advantage. Note also the Guy 'Indian chief' motif on the radiator cap. *Howard Butler*

Left: Many seaside operators extended the life of their vehicles by converting them to open-top configuration rather than consigning them to the scrapyard. Even in the war years East Kent was able to have a Park Royal body on the Guy Arab II chassis; BJG 339 was delivered in 1944 to utility specification and converted 15 years later to open-top, in which form it would survive until 1970. Note the typical Guy upswept front wing and the smart wheel-hub rings. *Rob Crouch*

Above: The 'FFN' batch of Park Royal-bodied Guy Arab IIIs enjoyed a creditable innings, a number being converted to open-top. In this form the Park Royal body retained its gracious lines, though it did not look its best following a period of hire in London during the early 1970s. Used for driver training from 1973, FFN 384 would finally be withdrawn in 1975, some 24 years after entering service. *Rob Crouch*

Converted to open-top in 1970, Guy Arab IV/Park Royal GFN 923 is seen shortly before withdrawal in 1973, its cream livery contrasting markedly with the standard application of red and cream seen on vehicles to either side. Behind is an AEC Regent V in the poppy-red livery soon to be seen throughout East Kent. *Rob Crouch*

At Christmas it was traditional for an East Kent double-deck vehicle to be repainted white. From 1962 to 1966 this role was performed by Park Royal-bodied Guy Arab

FFN 381 on Canterbury city service 27 in 1966. Within two years this vehicle would form part of the open-top fleet. *Howard Butler*

Left: Still fitted with the dependable Gardner 6LW engine, the final batch of Guy Arab IV buses, delivered in 1956/7, were more distinctive than their earlier cousins, the Park Royal body being more sharply raked at the front but still strikingly attractive, as exemplified by MFN 893. Fortunately sister vehicle MFN 888 survives in preservation to remind us of the heyday of East Kent. *Rob Crouch*

Above: By the time this view of Guy Arab IV/Park Royal MFN 887 was recorded in 1956 the destination screen had been masked to show the ultimate destination, giving the vehicle a make-do-and-mend appearance not in keeping with such a handsome vehicle. It is seen waiting to depart Canterbury bus station for Folkestone — a journey of just over an hour. *Rob Crouch*

This view at Westwood garage, Ramsgate, on the Isle of Thanet, taken in the late 1960s, could have been staged as a publicity shot, with perfect sunshine. In the late 1950s East Kent's double-deck allegiance changed from Guy to AEC, which manufacturer supplied 40 AEC Regent Vs. Most were delivered in 1959, but the vehicle depicted, PFN 843, was built in 1958 and was exhibited at that year's Commercial Motor Show. The bodywork was by Park Royal with a full front encasing the engine area, and remained a very attractive vehicle. *Rob Crouch*

This 1960s comparison of Park Royal-bodied AEC Regent V PFN 854 with Guy Arab III FFN 365 shows just how vertical the former type's bodywork was at the front. It shows just how smart East Kent's livery was, no matter what type of bus it was applied to, and the wheel ring and painted hub top off the effect perfectly. With further half-cabs visible in the background, this is a perfect snapshot of the days when classic buses ruled supreme in this part of the world. *Rob Crouch*

Above: Route 52 was one of the main trunk services between Ramsgate and Margate. Its route took it past Thanet garage, where this view was taken. Park Royal-bodied AEC Regent V PFN 851 dates from 1959 and looks immaculate in the spring sunshine with full informative destination display. *Rob Crouch*

Right: On a bright summer's day in June 1973, Park Royal-bodied AEC Regent Vs PFN 874 and YJG 810 are seen at Canterbury bus station. There is a three-year span between these two vehicles (1959-1962). The more handsome vehicle has to be PFN 874. Because of the registration number make-up, vehicles from this batch were nicknamed 'Puffins'. *John Bishop / Online Transport Archive*

Above: A number of the 'PFN' class of the AEC Regents were converted to permanent open-top. They were of a high standard enhanced by the livery and decal advertising route 69. As can be seen in this view taken at Westwood garage, Ramsgate, in July 1974, the poppy-red livery was encroaching fast; however, PFN 853 stands defiantly with dark red wheels. Note that Larry Grayson is appearing at the Ramsgate Winter Gardens. 'Shut that door!'. *John Bishop / Online Transport Archive*

Right: In August 1974, open-top Park Royal-bodied AEC Regent V PFN 853 was caught on Margate promenade on route 69 to Birchington in glorious sunshine with a respectable load. By the time this view was taken it had gained an NBC grey rear wheel. This particular bus was converted to open-top in July 1972.
John Bishop / Online Transport Archive

Left: The livery worn here by PFN 851 is not dissimilar in shade to that used today by Arriva. By October 1973, when this photograph was taken at Dover Port, the bus had been working for Townsend Thoresen for over two years. It would not be withdrawn until the end of the decade, some 20 years after entering service with East Kent. *John Bishop / Online Transport Archive*

Above: Park Royal-bodied AEC Regent V YJG 812, new in April 1962, has just arrived at Canterbury bus station from Deal on route 13. Having discharged his passengers, the conductor makes a hasty exit to the office to the right while the driver prepares to park the vehicle in the centre of the bus station for a well-earned break. YJG 812 would end its days as a driver-trainer vehicle. *Howard Butler*

Left: In 1962, specifically for route 129 in Dover, East Kent purchased three AEC Bridgemasters with Park Royal bodies, one of which, YJG 808, is depicted outside Dover garage. These looked more in proportion than their high-bridge cousins. They lasted only ten years before being withdrawn in 1972. *Rob Crouch*

Above: In this mid-1960s view in Dover town centre, one can draw a comparison between the height of the two Park Royal bodies, AEC Bridgemaster YJG 808 being much lower in height. At this moment in time the bus looks somewhat less cared for than the Park Royal-bodied AEC Regent V behind. The outbound journey of this bus's dedicated route 129 is underway, which will take it to St Radigunds. *Rob Crouch*

Left: When this portrait of AFN 771B was taken in March 1966, the AEC Regent V was a mere two years old. Pencester Road bus station would always be a marvellous place for photography, especially in the late afternoon, as shown here with the famous Dover Castle looking majestically over the town. *Howard Butler*

Above: This view of Park Royal-bodied AEC Regent V AFN 782B, dating from 1964, highlights how the rich red and cream of the East Kent livery looks on an otherwise unattractive Park Royal body. The polished chrome on the front offside wheel accentuates the finish and pride the company gave the vehicle. Note the Park Royal-bodied AEC Reliance in Skyways livery. *Howard Butler*

Left: The later Park Royal AEC Regent V deliveries were not on the same order of attractiveness as the 'PFNs'. However, the livery did enhance the bodywork, as seen in this June 1973 view of GJG 746D at Dover garage in June 1973. The offside advert on the AEC Regent V behind may herald the advent of the National Bus Company, but there is still pride felt by the East Kent Road Car Co, as evidenced by the staff, resplendent in their uniforms. *John Bishop / Online Transport Archive*

Above: The venue for this bleak view in the late 1960s is a cold Ashford with the Maidstone & District garage on the right. Taking centre stage is 1966 Park Royal-bodied AEC Regent V GJG 735D on local route 121. Park Royal-bodied AEC Reliance WFN 503 stands in the East Kent yard at the front of the garage. *Howard Butler*

36   Park Royal-bodied AEC Regent V AFN 778B, dating from 1964, is seen on a bright sunny day in July 1973 on Ashford town service 502 to Stanhope. This and three other buses had their seating capacity reduced to 70 by the fitment of a luggage pen, primarily for town services 501 and 502. *John Bishop / Online Transport Archive*

Seen on the Isle of Thanet on a private working in July 1974 is Park Royal-bodied AEC Regent V GJG 735D, dating from 1966. The only factor spoiling an otherwise perfect view is the National Bus Company-specification grey rear nearside wheel.

The bright yellow Mk I Ford Escort was new at the time and would look a winner at any rally today. Note in the background the heavy cast East Kent bus stop, now sought after by collectors. *John Bishop / Online Transport Archive*

Left: In 1969 East Kent turned to the Daimler Fleetline with Park Royal bodywork. RFN 958G shows off its well-proportioned body in the early 1970s at Thanet garage. *Rob Crouch*

Above: By the early 1970s the unreliability of rear-engined buses was well documented, as demonstrated by engineless RFN 966G, photographed on a wet 19 March 1975. National Bus Company poppy-red livery would soon be applied, but for now the only evidence of corporate identity is the advertising, which adorned many NBC buses some 30 years ago. *John Bishop / Online Transport Archive*

Left: Despite dating from 1948, the Park Royal-bodied Dennis Lancet still used prewar technology, the ruggedness of which possibly accounted for the buses' long lives in regular service with East Kent. Although updated mechanically during their careers, they never lost their classic appeal. They lasted until 1968, CJG 989 ending up as a towing vehicle before unfortunately being scrapped. *Rob Crouch*

Above: Seen at Canterbury bus station in the mid-1960s is Park Royal-bodied Dennis Lancet III CFN 123, one of a batch of 60 delivered between 1947 and 1949. This vehicle achieved 20 years of service before being sold and converted for non-PSV use at Dover Docks. *Howard Butler*

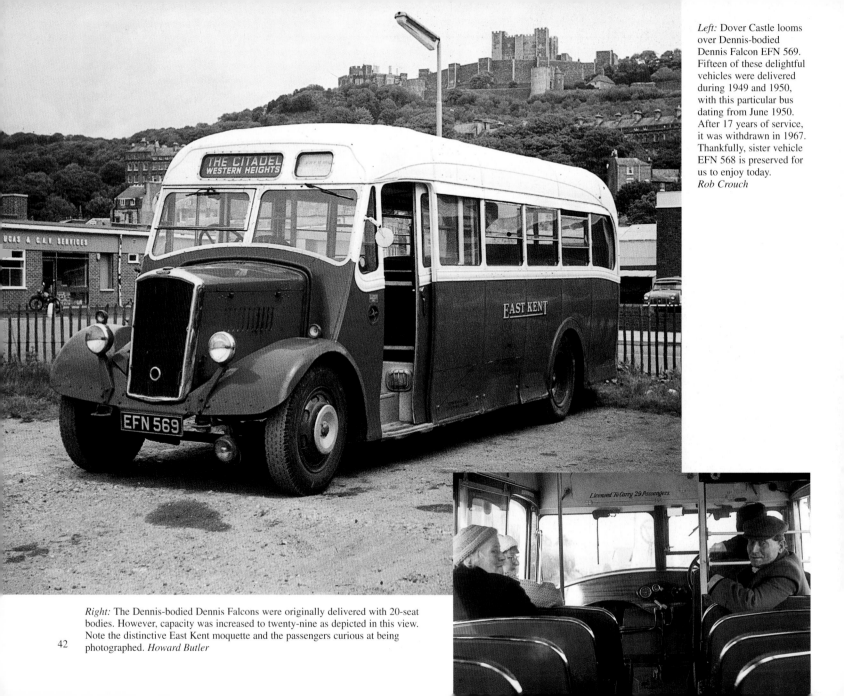

Left: Dover Castle looms over Dennis-bodied Dennis Falcon EFN 569. Fifteen of these delightful vehicles were delivered during 1949 and 1950, with this particular bus dating from June 1950. After 17 years of service, it was withdrawn in 1967. Thankfully, sister vehicle EFN 568 is preserved for us to enjoy today. *Rob Crouch*

Right: The Dennis-bodied Dennis Falcons were originally delivered with 20-seat bodies. However, capacity was increased to twenty-nine as depicted in this view. Note the distinctive East Kent moquette and the passengers curious at being photographed. *Howard Butler*

During the mid-1960s, a casual look in the bus station at Deal would often reveal a rebuilt Park Royal-bodied Dennis Lancet III such as CFN 116. Delivered in 1949 as a half-cab, the Lancet arguably looked old before its time. With the need to economise and the introduction of OMO (one-man operation), a number of this batch were rebuilt frontally for the purpose by Roe during 1959, allowing them another seven years' service. During this time the coalmines were still in use and route 76 serviced the area around Betteshanger colliery. *John Bishop / Online Transport Archive*

Above left: The Weymann-bodied AEC Reliances were the backbone of the Rye–Hastings services of East Kent, as shown by KFN 244 at Fairlight. Seen in the late 1960s, KFN 244 would soldier on until 1973 before being withdrawn and scrapped in 1974. The shelter by the Fairlight stores deserves a mention, proudly proclaiming 'East Kent Passenger Shelter'. The boy looking on will now be middle-aged, but time stands still in this view. *Rob Crouch*

Below left: An interesting photograph of Ore garage, which was built in 1960 but closed in 1969 when East Kent's services in Hastings were transferred to Maidstone & District. The building now forms part of a light industrial unit.

However, let us go back to the mid-1960s when this photograph was taken and examine the two vehicles. Compare the coach dual-purpose livery on the 'TFN'-class coach to the standard bus liveried 'KFN'-class bus. Even the lamp is painted in East Kent deep red. *Rob Crouch*

Above: We have reached journey's end at Pett Level on half-hourly service 128 from Hastings — you can't get much closer to the sea than this stop! Weymann-bodied AEC Reliance KFN 244, dating from 1955, lays over for a short time at an East Kent parking area with typical signs and timetable of the period. The vehicle served the company well, not being retired until 1973. *Rob Crouch*

In this patriotic view, with the Union Jack flying above Ricemans store at Canterbury bus station in June 1973, are three traditionally-liveried East Kent vehicles, including LJG 306, a single-deck Weymann-bodied AEC Reliance. There were 62 of these vehicles, delivered between 1955 and 1956 and registered in the KFN and LJG series respectively. These would prove to be fine workhorses, many seeing over 20 years of service. For LJG 306, however, 1973 would prove to be its last year. *John Bishop / Online Transport Archive*

The setting for this view of Marshall-bodied AEC Reliance DJG 355C is Deal bus station on local route 82. In 1965, when this vehicle was delivered, the holding company for East Kent was the British Electric Traction Company (BET). Its influence was in the style of bodywork for single-deck vehicles, which became known as the BET Federation design. The red front dome around the destination screen enhanced the effect, but upon repainting would be in cream.
Howard Butler

Standing serenely in the summer sun at Folkestone bus station is Marshall-bodied
AEC Reliance KJG 571E. The batch was soon converted for one-man operation
(OMO) but had a comparatively short life, being withdrawn in 1978. *Howard Butler*

Inside Ashford garage we see Marshall-bodied Bedford VAS1 KJG 104E, which was delivered in 1967 and is seen in traditional bus livery with destination screen set for its local Ashford route. These vehicles did not have as lengthy a service period as the Dennis Falcons they replaced, being withdrawn in 1975. *John Bishop / Online Transport Archive*

Above: By the time KJG 572E, a Marshall-bodied AEC Reliance, was seen at Canterbury bus station on 2 May 1973, the fleet name had been replaced with the National Bus Company logo above the front nearside window. This left a blank space and gave an odd appearance. The roof dome around the destination screen had been repainted red, and the vehicle had gained 'Pay on Entry' signs. *Dave Warren*

Right: BET Federation-designed Marshall-bodied AEC Swift RJG 201G is shown to good effect with shining hub rings and chrome surrounds to the headlights. The batch RJG 200-9G was delivered in June 1969 for OMO working, with a sign that illuminated below the front windscreen. *Rob Crouch*

Above: In June 1973, Marshall-bodied AEC Swift VJG 199J looked resplendent in traditional livery when compared with the vehicles either side at Ashford garage. It was delivered in early 1971 and was only two years old when seen here. *John Bishop / Online Transport Archive*

Right: In 1971, East Kent acquired 30 eight-year-old Marshall-bodied Leyland Leopards, 265-89 AUF and 100-4 CUF, from Southdown Motor Services. The chassis was alien to the engineers, the company being used to the AEC marque. They definitely looked the part in East Kent livery, however, as shown by this view of 284 AUF at Hythe in May 1973. *John Bishop / Online Transport Archive*

Left: In May 1973 ex-Southdown Marshall-bodied Leyland Leopard 281 AUF is seen at Folkestone bound for Hythe on route 103. There is no mistaking the characteristic Southdown 'V' in the beading below the windscreen where the 'Southdown' badge was once secured. Note the cast East Kent bus stop. *John Bishop / Online Transport Archive*

Above: With a backdrop of building work opposite the Folkestone bus station, ex-Southdown Marshall-bodied Leyland Leopard 281 AUF collects passengers in June 1975, beneath a No Entry sign exempting East Kent vehicles. By the time this picture was taken, the majority of the fleet had been repainted in National Bus Company poppy red, but other than grey-painted wheels, 281 AUF was still in traditional livery and wore proper fleetnames. The bus stops, however, had succumbed to the NBC design. *John Bishop / Online Transport Archive*

55

In November and December 1971, 12 Alexander Y-type-bodied AEC Swifts were based at Dover for the town services. Proud to be wearing its fine livery, YJG 591K stands near the Dover garage. The British cars seen in this view deserve a mention with a Vauxhall Victor to the right and an Austin A35 Countryman in the background. *Rob Crouch*

Although the AEC Swift would continue to be produced, these would be the last to be acquired by East Kent. These vehicles were among the last to wear the classic livery from new, but by the time this photograph of YJG 588K was taken in the early 1970s, the fleetname had been covered over, giving an ungainly appearance. *Rob Crouch*

Above left: For many enthusiasts this picture of JG 9938, taken at Folkestone in June 1965, conjures up a vision of the perfect restoration. The vehicle is a Park Royal-bodied Leyland Tiger TS8 with a design not dissimilar to the Dennis Lancet and post-war Leyland PS1 coaches. The fact that it was transferred into the non-service fleet to perform duties as a mobile office was its salvation, and it is now on the rally circuit for all to enjoy. *John Bishop / Online Transport Archive*

Left: Park Royal-bodied Dennis Lancet EFN 587 dates from 1950, and with the imminent advent of the underfloor engine coaches, would be out of date within 12 months. Nevertheless, they would serve the company well, with an in-depth feel of

quality and pride. The beading and company name on the radiator gave these vehicles a certain edge over the competition. This particular vehicle enjoyed a long working life and spent its final years as a snowplough before being withdrawn in 1969. *Howard Butler*

Above: At the eastern end of the seafront at Hastings coach park are two classic East Kent coaches. Looking the true heavyweight coach of the time, with its bright aluminium trim that enhanced its curved bodywork, stands FFN 452, a Park Royal-bodied Leyland Royal Tiger dating from 1951. Behind is a Duple Ambassador 'HFN' Royal Tiger. *Howard Butler*

59

A classic view of a classic vehicle: Duple Ambassador-bodied Leyland Royal Tiger HFN 1 emerging onto the seafront in Bexhill-on-Sea. Delivered in 1953, it still looks resplendent in its East Kent livery some 12 years on. Justifiably, the driver in his summer uniform looks proud. Both Leyland Royal Tigers would be withdrawn from service in 1967, ending their days as contractor's vehicles with Wimpey. *Rob Crouch*

This photograph of HJG 16 was taken on 12 April 1971, capturing the final guise of a superb-looking coach. The bodywork is Duple's Ambassador design, mounted on the Dennis Lancet IV chassis. Dennis referred to this as the Lancet UF type, the letters denoting an underfloor engine. Delivered in 1954 in East Kent red and cream, these 30 vehicles confirmed the company's loyalty to Dennis for its coaching requirements. Only in 1970 were examples painted in blue and white for Seaspeed transfer work from Dover Priory station to the hovercraft. *Dave Warren*

Above: In 1957, East Kent took into stock 12 Beadle-bodied AEC Reliances, MJG 41-52, for touring work. Their graceful lines were enhanced further by the application of East Kent colours. When delivered, they only seated 32 passengers but were rebuilt to seat 34 in 1963. The large shield/coat of arms on the front was used for Canterbury city tours. *Howard Butler*

Right: A Dennis Lancet is bound for Dover on the newly-opened M2 on a bright summer's day during the mid-1960s. Work is still being carried out and some adventurous motorists can be seen in the distance. Dennis of Guildford classified this underfloor-engined type as the Lancet UF. The bodywork was the Duple Ambassador and looked classy with the decal proudly displayed. *Howard Butler*

Above: Although these three Beadle-bodied buses, KFN 250-2, looked similar to the 'NFN' and 'MJG' AEC Reliances, they also employed the Commer TS3 two-stroke diesel engine and were built in 1955 with a semi-chassisless body. The body structure was, therefore, a substantial part of the strength. These three vehicles were initially used as coaches before being relegated to stage carriage operation. They were withdrawn from service in 1969 and 1970 and are seen in the depot yard at Herne Bay. *Rob Crouch*

Right: In 1957, East Kent turned to Beadle of Dartford to body a further intake of AEC Reliances; MJG 286 is an example, emerging from Canterbury bus station in June 1973 whilst on stage-carriage work. When delivered, these 15 vehicles were used on coach duties with MJG 286 wearing the Europabus livery. The class would perform a dual-purpose role throughout their lives, and this vehicle lasted until 1974. *John Bishop / Online Transport Archive*

The Beadle-bodied AEC Reliances of 1957 did not share the same elegance as the Beadle-bodied touring coaches of the 'MJG' class, though they had mechanical features in common. Seen at Rye station in the mid-1960s working the local route to Hastings, NFN 342 shares the road with a Weymann-bodied AEC Reliance, KFN 215. The roadside advertisement reads: 'The stamp of quality depends on you', encouraging the public to buy British — something regrettably practised much less nowadays. *Howard Butler*

Right: A delightful view of Beadle-bodied AEC Reliance MJG 44 and Harrington-bodied Ford Thames TJG 440 at Farthing Corner Service Station, Gillingham, Kent, in the mid-1960s. This nearside view of the Beadle coachwork shows just how elegant these vehicles were. *Howard Butler*

Right: Thomas Harrington of Hove in East Sussex ceased production in 1966, having built many attractive vehicles. However, this was not one of their best. The body design was the 'Crusader' and would be the sole representative in the East Kent fleet. The body was mounted on a Ford chassis, registered TJG 440, and is seen in the mid-1960s at Westwood depot, Ramsgate. TJG 440 was delivered in 1960 and would see 12 years' service before being withdrawn in 1972. The condition and brilliant-white headrests are what one expected from East Kent Road Car Company. *Rob Crouch*

Against a backdrop of advertisements in Ramsgate we see a dual-purpose Park Royal-bodied AEC Reliance, TFN 434, on 28 January 1975. This year marked the end of traditional red and cream in favour of poppy red. This vehicle was withdrawn later in the year and scrapped in 1976, a sad end for a fine vehicle that was once the pride of the East Kent fleet when delivered in 1960. *John Bishop / Online Transport Archive*

Three Park Royal-bodied AEC Reliances are seen at Dover Priory station in June 1973, and all are wearing different liveries. The centre vehicle, TFN 418, sports the traditional red and cream while TFN 411 and 402 wear variations of the Seaspeed Hovercraft livery. It is refreshing that the paint shop retained the mouldings on the fronts of these vehicles, enhancing their appearance.
John Bishop

Left: In 1962 East Kent took delivery of 20 handsome Park Royal-bodied AEC Reliances, registered 519-38 FN. One of them was 536 FN, depicted in the mid-1960s. After ten years' service, these vehicles were rebodied by Plaxton with Panorama Elite coachwork, thereby extending their lives considerably. *Rob Crouch*

Above: Park Royal-bodied AEC Reliance 526 FN, dating from 1962, is seen at Folkestone surrounded by AEC Regent Vs and a lone Guy Arab to the left. Carrying Skyways contract livery for the air service from Lympne, it provided the many services for contracts in connection with cross-channel traffic. *Rob Crouch*

In the mid-1960s East Kent's front-line coaches were Park Royal-bodied AEC Reliances such as DJG 631C, seen loading by the pier at Eastbourne in June 1976; note the Eastbourne Borough inspector hurrying the throngs of passengers towards the endless flow of coaches leaving in the late afternoon. Delivered in 1965 as one of a batch of 26, this vehicle would remain in service until 1978. *John Bishop / Online Transport Archive*

When this shot was taken on 26 May 1969, Victoria Coach Station was a Mecca for coaches in a variety of liveries, including this 1966 East Kent Park Royal-bodied AEC Reliance, GJG 641D in Skyways Coach Air Service livery. There is no mistaking the East Kent style, albeit in contract livery. *Dave Warren*

Left: 'Not the heyday, surely!' However, it does show how elegant the Park Royal design was. AEC Reliance DJG 610C was delivered in 1965, and when photographed on 25 January 1975 at Dover, was about to be repainted into the National Bus Company livery. Withdrawn in 1978, it would be exported to Jamaica. *John Bishop*

Right: A threatening cloud formation gives a dramatic backdrop to this view of Duple Commander-bodied AEC Reliance AFN 490B at Gillingham in 1964, when virtually brand new. Used initially on tours, it only seated 34 passengers. Later downgraded, along with the rest of the batch, it would survive to receive National white livery. *Howard Butler*

Right: Seen on a murky day in 1967 is a Mercedes-Benz O302 demonstrator, appropriately registered OLH 302E, on the L2 coach service between London and the Isle of Thanet. None were acquired, East Kent continuing to standardise on the AEC Reliance for its coaching requirements until the mid-1970s. *Rob Crouch*

This mid-1960s view demonstrates contemporary trends in coach design, fashion and even architecture. Although holidaymakers were increasingly heading abroad, they still made use of coaches to convey them to airports or seaports. AFN 495B, a sparkling Duple Commander-bodied AEC Reliance with white headrests, is waiting outside the East Kent Road Car headquarters, a brutalist construction totally out of keeping with the adjacent buildings in Canterbury. *Howard Butler*

Give a Plaxton Panorama body, already attractive, a coat of East Kent red and cream and the vehicle becomes positively outstanding. Delivered in 1970, VJG 474J is seen at the Hoverport in Calais on 15 June 1971, showing off its well-proportioned lines.

As can be seen, black-on-white numberplates had been introduced to British vehicles and were beginning to spread to the East Kent bus and coach fleet; while somewhat stark, they do not detract particularly from the coach's overall appeal. *Dave Warren*

Recovery vehicles are easy to photograph in depot yards but not on the road. Ex-War Department vehicles were plentiful after hostilities and East Kent took the opportunity to acquire this 1944 AEC Matador in 1948. The vehicle went on to provide sterling service until its retirement in 1974. *Howard Butler*

East Kent is notorious for heavy snow, and two Canterbury-based Park Royal Dennis Lancet III coaches with Park Royal bodywork, EFN 587 and 588, were used as snowploughs between 1962 and 1968 on hire to Kent County Council.

EFN 587 is seen fitted with its plough and ready for action — very much a fall from grace. Both vehicles would be scrapped in 1970. *Howard Butler*

Left: As East Kent's classic red and cream had succumbed to NBC corporate poppy red, so disappeared the latter livery in turn when Stagecoach purchased East Kent in 1993 and imposed its white and stripes scheme. Still, the 90th anniversary of the East Kent Road Car Co's formation fell in 2006, for which four contemporary Stagecoach buses donned traditional liveries. Northern Counties-bodied Volvo Olympian 16246 is seen in May 2005 at Hastings bus rally. *John Bishop / Online Transport Archive*

Below: At the Hastings bus rally the opportunity was taken to pose Stagecoach's four repainted buses in their local liveries. Here two East Kent Olympians — Leyland 14821 and Volvo 16246 — take centre stage, flanked by Volvo B10Ms painted in the liveries of Maidstone & District and Hastings Tramways, to celebrate 100 years since the first Hastings tram took to the road. *John Bishop / Online Transport Archive*